BIRDS

Izzi Howell

Published in 2018 by **Windmill Books**, an Imprint of Rosen Publishing
29 East 21st Street, New York, NY 10010

Editor: Izzi Howell
Design: Clare Nicholas
Other illustrations: Stefan Chabluk
Consultant: Kate Ruttle

Picture and illustration credits: Corbis: Tui De Roy/Minden Pictures 19; iStock: evil_ss 4tl, Guillermo Perales Gonzalez 4br, Jonathan Woodcock 7b, JK-photo 9, Kenneth Canning 13, Anoliso1 17t, KeithSzafranski 17b, Craig Dingle 20; Shutterstock: Donjiy cover, Ondrej Prosicky title page and 12, Jesse Nguyen 4tr, john michael evan potter 4br, Kateryna Larina 5, MagMac83 6, Paul Reeves Photography 7, Nagel Photography 8, Andrzej Kubik 10, duangnapa_b 11, Stephanie Periquet 14t, David Steele 14b, Sergey Ryzhov 15, Cheryl E. Davis 16, Wollertz 18, feathercollector 21.

Cataloging-in-Publication Data
Names: Howell, Izzi.
Title: Birds / Izzi Howell.
Description: New York : Windmill Books, 2017. Series: Fact finders: animals Includes index.
Identifiers: ISBN 9781499483062 (pbk.) ISBN 9781499483017 (library bound) ISBN 9781499482928 (6 pack)
Subjects: LCSH: Birds--Juvenile literature.
Classification: LCC QL676.2 H69 2017 DDC 598--dc23

Manufactured in China
CPSIA Compliance Information: Batch #BS17WM: For Further Information contact
Rosen Publishing, New York, New York at 1-800-237-9932

FACT FINDER

There is a question for you to answer on each spread in this book. You can check your answers on page 24.

CONTENTS

WHAT IS A BIRD?

Birds are a group of animals that are similar to each other in certain ways. Birds have wings and they are covered in feathers. Young birds (called chicks) hatch from eggs.

Lorikeets, cardinals, cranes, and gulls are all different types of birds. Which country do you think has the gray crowned crane as its national bird?

lorikeet

cardinal

gray crowned crane

yellow-legged gull

Birds are **warm-blooded** animals. This means that they can control the temperature of their bodies. In hot weather, birds lose heat by **panting** or by spreading out their wings.

The flamingo often stands on one leg, so that only one of its legs is in the cold water. This helps it to stay warm.

FACT FINDER

Flamingos are pink because they eat a lot of **algae**, which contain a natural pink **pigment**. If a flamingo stopped eating algae, its feathers would turn white!

HABITAT

Birds live in different **habitats**, from rain forests and lakes to deserts and oceans. Some birds, such as parrots, live high in the branches of trees. Other birds, such as ostriches, never leave the ground.

Many birds, such as pigeons, live in towns and cities. What is another name for white pigeons?

Some birds, such as gulls, spend much of their time near water. However, almost all birds come onto land to lay their eggs and take care of their chicks.

Some birds, such as this barn swallow, **migrate** to warm habitats during the winter months. They return to colder habitats in spring to lay their eggs.

FACT FINDER

The Arctic tern travels over 50,000 miles (80,000 km) every year, migrating from the Arctic to Antarctica and back again.

BREATHING

nostril

All birds need to breathe air. When a bird breathes in, its **air sacs** and **lungs** take **oxygen** from the air and send it around their bodies.

The peacock, like most birds, can breathe through its mouth or its nostrils.

Having air sacs as well as lungs means that a bird can take in more oxygen from the air than other types of animal. This means that birds can fly high in the sky, where there is less oxygen than there is on the ground.

The common crane breathes through its air sacs and lungs to give it enough oxygen to fly at heights of up to 33,000 feet (10,000 m)!

FACT FINDER

The kiwi is the only bird with nostrils at the end of its long **beak**. Most birds have nostrils on top of their beaks. Which country does the kiwi come from?

WINGS

Birds use their wings to fly. When a bird pushes air down with its wings, it moves higher. Birds move forwards by pushing air backwards with their wings.

All birds have wings, but some birds, such as ostriches, can't fly. What other kinds of birds are flightless?

FACT FINDER

Instead of flying, ostriches use their long legs to run at speeds of up to 40 miles (64 km) per hour!

Birds' wings are covered in soft feathers. This smooth **surface** helps birds to move their wings quickly through the air.

Birds twist the tips of their wings to change the direction they are flying in.